REASONS YOU SHOULD(N'T) LOVE ME

by Amy Trigg

SAMUEL FRENCH

FOR AMATEUR PRODUCTION ENQUIRIES

UNITED KINGDOM AND WORLD
EXCLUDING NORTH AMERICA
licensing@concordtheatricals.co.uk

020-7054-7200

Each title is subject to availability from Concord Theatricals, depending upon country of performance.

REASONS YOU SHOULD(N'T) LOVE ME was the winner of the 2020 Women's Prize for Playwriting, founded by Ellie Keel Productions and Paines Plough and was first performed at the Kiln Theatre on 21st May 2021.

The Women's Prize for Playwriting, Paines Plough, 45North and Kiln Theatre present:

REASONS YOU SHOULD(N'T) LOVE ME

Written and Performed by Amy Trigg

Director – Charlotte Bennett

Designer – Jean Chan

Lighting Designer – Guy Hoare

Sound Designer – Elena Peña

Associate Director – Hana Pascal Keegan

Production Manager – Nicki Brown

Deputy Production Manager – Scott Handley

Company Stage Manager – Alex Constantin

Deputy Stage Manager – Sophie Rubenstein

Assistant Stage Manager – Ella Saunders

Wardrobe Manager – Megan Keegan

Show Crew – Kieran Watson

Lighting Operator – Federica Spada

Production Electrician – Steve Andrews

Production Sound – Jon Sealey, Chris Payne

Lighting Programmer – Tamykha Patterson

Set Built By – Illusion Design and Construct, Kiln Theatre Workshop

CAST AND CREATIVE

WRITTEN AND PERFORMED BY
AMY TRIGG | JUNO

Amy trained at Mountview Academy of Theatre Arts.

Theatre includes: *The Taming of the Shrew* and *Measure for Measure* (RSC), *Sadler's Wells Takeover Weekend* (River Stage at The National Theatre); *The Joy of Dance* (Lyric Hammersmith); *Fusion* (Sadler's Wells); *The Sonnet Walks* (Shakespeare's Globe); *Shakespeare within the Abbey* (Shakespeare's Globe at Westminster Abbey); *Goth Weekend* (Stephen Joseph Theatre/ Live Theatre); *A Brief History of Plays* (Stephen Joseph Theatre), *Tommy* (New Wolsey/Ramps on the Moon); *The Glass Menagerie* (Nottingham Playhouse); *Philip Pullman's Grimm Tales* (Digital Piece – Unicorn Theatre).

Televison includes: *Feel Good* (Netflix); *Unprecedented: Going Forward* (20th Century Films/BBC); *Doctors* (BBC); *Stella* (Tidy Productions Limited).

Film includes: *Mamma Mia! Here We Go Again;* Short: *Pas de Deux.*

Writing work: *Reasons You Should(n't) Love Me* (joint winner of the inaugural Women's Prize for Playwriting 2020); Amy's essay *An Ode to Improv (and Poehler and Fey)* features in the book *Feminist's Don't Wear Pink (and other lies)*; *The Rebrand* (one-woman sketch, winner of the Colchester New Comedian of the Year 2016). Amy is currently a writer for the upcoming BBC series *Ralph and Katie* and is developing original projects for stage and screen. She has been part of the Royal Court Introduction to Playwriting Group 2020/21, BBC Drama Room 2020/21, BBC Writers Access Group 2020/21 and 4Screenwriting 2021.

CHARLOTTE BENNETT | DIRECTOR

Charlotte Bennett is Joint Artistic Director of Paines Plough. Previously she was Associate Director at Soho Theatre where she led the new writing department, developing artists and commissions and programming the upstairs studio. For Paines Plough she has directed *Run Sister Run* by Chloë Moss. For Soho Theatre she has directed *Whitewash* by Gabriel Bisset-Smith, *Happy Hour* by Jack Rooke and led playwriting competition the Verity Bargate Award.

Prior to this she was Artistic Director of Forward Theatre Project; an artists' collective she founded. For Forward Theatre Project she directed new plays, inspired by working with different communities around the UK, which toured nationally at venues including National Theatre, York Theatre Royal, Northern Stage, Derby Theatre, Live Theatre and The Lowry. As a freelance director she has worked extensively for Open Clasp Theatre Company, creating new plays inspired by marginalised women. She also held the role of Producer for theatre company RashDash where she toured experimental new theatre around the UK.

JEAN CHAN | DESIGNER

Jean Chan studied at the Royal Welsh College of Music and Drama, graduating in 2008 with a BA Hons Degree in Theatre Design. She went on to work as a resident designer, part of the Royal Shakespeare Company's Trainee Design Programme 2008-2009. In 2009 she won the Linbury Prize for Stage Design.

Designs include: *A Midsummer Night's Dream* (Shakespeare's Globe Theatre); *Dick Whittington, Jack and the Beanstalk* (Lyric Hammersmith); *The Hired Man, Much Ado about Nothing* (Queen's Theatre, Hornchurch); *Working* (Southwark Playhouse); *Plastic* (Theatre Royal Bath); *Ticking* (Trafalgar Studios); *The Witches, James and the Giant Peach, The BFG* (Dundee Rep); *Jumpy, Hedda Gabler* (The Royal Lyceum, Edinburgh); *The Season Ticket* (Pilot Theatre and Northern Stage); *Cyrano De Bergerac* (The Royal & Derngate and Northern Stage); *Mother Courage, Bordergames, Tonypandemonium* (National Theatre Wales); *This Land* (Pentabus Theatre and Salisbury Playhouse); *The Husbands, For Once, Mayfair* (Kali Theatre and Pentabus Theatre); *The Hairy Ape, The Irish Giant, The Seagull* (Southwark

Playhouse); *Hamlet Young People's Shakespeare* (Royal Shakespeare Company); *The Garbage King* (The Unicorn Theatre).

Costume designs include: *Knight's Tale* (Toho Theatre, Japan); *The Grinning Man* (Trafalgar Studios and Bristol Old Vic); *Aladdin* (Lyric Hammersmith); *Lionboy* (Complicite).

Associate designs include: *Les Liaisons Dangereuses* (Theatre Cocoon, Japan); *The James Plays* (National Theatre Scotland and Great Britain); *Lionboy* (Complicite); *Five Guys Named Moe* (Underbelly and Theatre Royal Stratford East); *Monsters* (Arcola Theatre).

GUY HOARE | LIGHTING DESIGNER

Guy is an associate artist at Wilton's Music Hall.

For Kiln Theatre: *Wife*

Theatre includes: *Sea Wall/A Life* (Broadway); *Julie, The Deep Blue Sea, Here We Go, Strange Interlude* (National Theatre); *Jesus Hopped The A Train, Wings, A Doll's House, World Factory, Far Away* (Young Vic); *One For Sorrow, NSFW, In Basildon* (Royal Court); *Roots, Serenading Louie, Be Near Me* (Donmar Warehouse); *Little Revolution, A Delicate Balance, Waste* (Almeida); *Clarence Darrow* (The Old Vic); *The Father, Othello* (West End); *Peter Pan* (National Theatre of Scotland); *Sleeping Beauty* (Citizens Theatre); *Cock* (Chichester Festival Theatre); *Macbeth, As You Like It* (West Yorkshire Playhouse); *West Side Story, Grease* (Curve); *Assassins* (Crucible, Sheffield), *A Christmas Carol* (Birmingham Repertory Theatre); *Kes* (Liverpool Playhouse); *Going Dark* (Sound & Fury).

Designs for dance include: Arthur Pita's *The Metamorphosis* (Royal Opera House/Joyce Theatre, New York | Southbank Award for Dance) and Mark Bruce's *Dracula* (Wilton's Music Hall | Southbank Award for Dance), and various pieces worldwide for – amongst others – Rafael Bonachela, Christopher Bruce, Dan Daw, Shobana Jeyasingh, Akram Khan and Alexander Whitley. He also designed international tours of *Mischief* for Theatre Rites and several cross-artform works for Gandini Juggling.

Opera includes: *The Firework-Maker's Daughter* (Royal Opera House); *Jakob Lenz* (ENO); *American Lulu* (Bregenz Festival); *King Priam* (Olivier Award for Outstanding Achievement in Opera), *Paul Bunyan* (English Touring Opera).

ELENA PEÑA | SOUND DESIGNER

For Kiln Theatre: *Snowflake, The Kilburn Passion, Arabian Nights.*

Theatre includes: *Open Mic* (English Touring Theatre & Soho Theatre); *Women of Troy* (LAMDA); *The Living Newspaper: Edition 2, seven methods of killing kylie jenner* (Royal Court); *Misty* (West End); *Going Through, Hir, Islands* (Bush Theatre); *Rockpool* (Audio) (Inspector Sands & Trigger); *We're Stuck!* (One Tenth Human); *The Astro Science Challenge: Live!* (Unlimited Theatre); *Rockets & Blue Lights, Mountains* (Royal Exchange); *Autoreverse, Boat* (Battersea Arts Centre); *Everything, Brainstorm* (National Theatre) (Company Three); *The Memory of Water* (Nottingham Playhouse); *The Remains of the Day* (Out of Joint/Royal & Derngate, Northampton); *Thick As Thieves* (Clean Break); *The Wizard of Oz* (Pitlochry Festival); *All of Me* (China Plate); *Double Vision* (Wales Millennium Centre); *The Caretaker* (Bristol Old Vic); *The Lounge* (Soho/Summer Hall, Edinburgh); *How I Hacked My Way Into Space* (Unlimited/UK tour); *Years of Sunlight* (Theatre503); *The Bear/The Proposal, Flashes* (Young Vic); *Sleepless* (Analogue/Staatstheater Mainz, Germany); *The Christians* (Traverse); *I Call My Brothers, The Iphigenia Quartet, Unbroken* (Gate); *Thebes Land, Ant Street, Brimstone & Treacle, Knives In Hens* (Arcola); *You Have Been Upgraded* (Unlimited/Science Museum); *Seochon Odyssey* (HiSeoul Festival, Korea); *Mass Observation* (Almeida.)

Dance includes: *Patrias, Quimeras* (Sadlers Wells/Paco Peña Flamenco Company).

Television/online includes: *Have Your Circumstances Changed?, Brainstorm, The Astro Science Challenge.*

Radio includes: *Rockets & Blue Lights* (Reduced Listening Company); *The Meet Cute, Twelve Years, Duchamps Urinal* (BBC).

Installation includes: *Have Your Circumstances Changed?, Yes These Eyes Are The Windows* (ArtAngel).

HANA PASCAL KEEGAN | ASSOCIATE DIRECTOR

Hana is a director, dramaturg and writer. She trained at Graeae Theatre (UK), Young Vic Directors Programme (UK), National Theatre Institute (USA), College Of The Atlantic (USA).

She's most recently been investigating virtual, augmented and mixed reality storytelling with Donmar Warehouse and NT Immersive Storytelling Studio.

Theatre includes: *All Of Us* (National Theatre); *Macbeth* (Chichester Festival Theatre); *Jellyfish* (National Theatre, Bush Theatre); *All My Sons* (The Old Vic); *Open Mic* (Soho Theatre, English Touring Theatre); *Crips Without Constraints* (Graeae).

A MESSAGE FROM ELLIE KEEL ON BEHALF OF THE PRODUCERS OF *REASONS YOU SHOULD(N'T) LOVE ME*

I'm writing this introduction from the corner of the rehearsal room for *Reasons You Should(n't) Love Me*. It's a rare visit because of COVID precautions, so it feels all the more exciting and special to be here, watching this production being brought to life by an exceptional team after a long wait and a challenging year.

In December 2020, after surpassing over 1,100 submissions to reach the shortlist, *Reasons You Should(n't) Love Me* was awarded one of two First Prizes of the inaugural Women's Prize for Playwriting. We founded The Women's Prize for Playwriting partly to dispel the myth that women can't – or don't – write 'big plays', and that 'big plays' always have large casts and overtly political themes. Fittingly, as one of the Prize's inaugural winners, *Reasons You Should(n't) Love Me* is a one-woman play with a big heart and a resounding message.

This production is a collaboration between four female-led organisations: Kiln Theatre, The Women's Prize for Playwriting, Paines Plough and 45North. The team effort involved in making the show feels particularly nourishing after a year of physical separation. As producers, we feel incredibly fortunate to be returning to live work with such a warm, life-affirming play. We hope and believe that it will bring the same joy, and more, to its long-awaited audiences.

Ellie Keel and all at **The Women's Prize for Playwriting**, **Charlotte Bennett**, **Katie Posner** and all at **Paines Plough**, **Jessica Rose McVay** and all at **45North**, and **Indhu Rubasingham**, **Daisy Heath** and all at **Kiln Theatre**.

The mission of **The Women's Prize for Playwriting** is to bring about gender parity in the writers of plays on national stages by finding and producing the best new plays by women in the UK and Ireland. In 2018, only 26% of new main-stage plays were written by women.

In 2020, its inaugural year, the Prize received 1,163 submissions. The Judging Panel awarded two First Prizes of £12,000 to *Reasons You Should(n't) Love Me* by Amy Trigg and *You Bury Me* by Ahlam.

The Prize is a collaboration between Ellie Keel Productions and Paines Plough.

Founder and Director: Ellie Keel

Co-founders (WPP) and Joint Artistic Directors (Paines Plough): Charlotte Bennett and Katie Posner

New Work Associate (Paines Plough): Phillippe Cato

Associate Producer (WPP): Gabrielle Leadbeater

Development Producer (WPP, 2020): Saxon Mudge

Publicist: Kate Morley PR

Principal Partner (2021): 45North

Official Publishing and Licensing Partner: Concord Theatricals Ltd

Founding Sponsor: PER People

In association with Sonia Friedman Productions

Judging Panel 2020: Adjoa Andoh, Monica Dolan, Sarah Frankcom, Ella Hickson, Mel Kenyon (Chair), Kate Pakenham, Maxine Peake, Indhu Rubasingham.

Judging Panel 2021:
Arifa Akbar, Mel Kenyon (Chair), Lucy Kirkwood, Jasmine Lee-Jones, Winsome Pinnock, Indhu Rubasingham, Jenny Sealey, Nina Steiger, Nicola Walker, Jodie Whittaker.

With thanks to Thomas Bailey, Mike Bartlett, Hugh Bonneville, Emma D'Arcy, David Edgar, Jessica Lazar, Joanna Lumley, Jerwood Space, Sir Ian McKellen, Gail McManus, Kate Mosse, the National Theatre, RB Films and Lucy Prebble.

For more information visit www.womensprizeforplaywriting.co.uk

Paines Plough

Paines Plough is the national theatre of new plays. A touring company dedicated entirely to developing and producing exceptional new writing to connect with artists and communities across the UK.

"The lifeblood of the UK's theatre ecosystem." **The Guardian**

Since 1974 Paines Plough has produced more than 200 new productions by world renowned playwrights including Sarah Kane, Mark Ravenhill, Dennis Kelly, Mike Bartlett, Kae Tempest and Vinay Patel and we tour our plays to over 40 places each year. We reach over 30,000 people annually from Cornwall to the Orkney Islands, in village halls, off Broadway and in our own pop-up theatre Roundabout.

"That noble company Paines Plough, de facto national theatre of new writing." **The Daily Telegraph**

Furthering our reach beyond theatre walls, our audio app COME TO WHERE I'M FROM hosts 180 original mini plays about home and our digital projects connect with audiences via WhatsApp, phone, email and even by post. Wherever you are, you can experience a Paines Plough Production.

"I think some theatre just saved my life." **@kate_clement on Twitter**

Paines Plough

2nd Floor, 10 Leake Street, London SE1 7NN

+ 44 (0)20 7240 4533

office@painesplough.com

www.painesplough.com

🐦 Follow @PainesPlough on Twitter

📷 Follow @painesplough on Instagram

📘 Like Paines Plough at facebook.com/PainesPloughHQ

G Donate to Paines Plough at justgiving.com/PainesPlough

Paines Plough Limited is a company limited by guarantee and a registered charity.

Registered Company no: 1165130

Registered Charity no: 267523

Supported by
**ARTS COUNCIL
ENGLAND**

 **45NORTH**

45North champions, develops, and produces outstanding work by female-identifying and non-binary artists. Founded in 2019 and led by the very best creative teams from a variety of performing and producing backgrounds, 45North continues to reinvest in emerging artists who are beginning and expanding their practices through our seed commission schemes.

45North commits to maintaining creative teams of no less than 75% female-identifying or non-binary people, working to bring inclusive and exciting new theatre and events to London, Edinburgh, across the UK and internationally. Based in Hackney, beginning in 2021 45North commits to reflecting our local demographic and hiring no less than 40% People of the Global Majority across our creative teams.

We take risks to challenge our ideas of self and the world in which we live. We encourage our audiences to do the same.

45North

Studio 44, Hackney Downs Studios, London E8 2BT

+44 (0)7709 246253

admin@forty-fivenorth.com

www.forty-fivenorth.com

Follow @forty_fivenorth on Twitter

Follow @forty_fivenorth on Instagram

Like 45North at facebook.com/45NorthProds

Donate to 45North at www.forty-fivenorth.com/support

45North Limited is a private company limited by shares.
Registered Company no: 12259182

"Kiln Theatre has revitalised the cultural life of Brent and brings world-class theatre at an affordable price to people from all walks of life." **Zadie Smith**

Kiln Theatre sits in the heart of Kilburn in Brent, a unique and culturally diverse area of London where over 140 languages are spoken. We are a newly refurbished, welcoming and proudly local venue, with an internationally acclaimed programme of world and UK premieres. Our work presents the world through a variety of lenses, amplifying unheard / ignored voices into the mainstream, exploring and examining the threads of human connection that cross race, culture and identity.

"This place was a special cocoon. Now she has grown and blossomed into a beautiful butterfly." **Sharon D Clarke**

We believe that theatre is for all and want everyone to feel welcome and entitled to call the Kiln their own. We are committed to nurturing the talent of young people and providing a platform for their voices to be heard.

"In 2020, a year like no other, Kiln Theatre not only enjoyed runs of critically acclaimed shows but also recommitted to its core mission – serving its local community. It is devoted to young people and has had Brent's recovery and renewal firmly at the heart of their initiatives." **Winner London Theatre of the Year, The Stage Awards**

We look forward to welcoming you to Kilburn.

We are so grateful to the thousands of people and organisations whose donations ensured that we could open again in 2021.

Without your support, we would not be here today.

Thank you.

KilnTheatre.com/Give

Kiln Theatre
269 Kilburn High Road, London, NW6 7JR
KilnTheatre.com / KilnCinema.com
Info@KilnTheatre.com
 @KilnTheatre / @KilnCinema

Registered Charity no: 1396429

PRODUCER CREDITS

THE WOMEN'S PRIZE FOR PLAYWRITING

Founder and Director
Ellie Keel

Associate Producer
Gabrielle Leadbeater

2021 Judging Panel
Arifa Akbar, Indhu Rubasingham, Winsome Pinnock, Jenny Sealey, Nicola Walker, Mel Kenyon, Lucy Kirkwood, Jasmine Lee-Jones, Nina Steiger, Jodie Whittaker

PAINES PLOUGH

Joint Artistic Directors and CEOs
Charlotte Bennett & Katie Posner

Executive Producer
Holly Gladwell

Technical Director
Colin Everitt

Finance Manager (Interim)
Gemma Grand

Producer
Matt Maltby

Associate Producer
Christabel Holmes

Marketing & Audience Development Manager
Jo Langdon

New Work Associate
Phillippe Cato

The Big Room Playwright Fellow
Vickie Donoghue

The Big Room Playwright Bursary Recipient
Ric Renton

Trainee Director
Kaleya Baxe

Trainee Producer
Ellen Larson

Marketing Trainee
Molly Goetzee

Board of Directors
Ankur Bahl, Corey Campbell, Kim Grant (Chair), Asma Hussain, Tarek Iskander, Olivier Pierre-Noël, Cindy Polemis, Carolyn Saunders, Laura Wade

45NORTH

Creative Director and CEO
Jessica Rose McVay

Creative Producer for Theatre
Emily Carewe

Creative Producer for Events
Charlie Lees-Massey

KILN THEATRE

Artistic Director
Indhu Rubasingham

Executive Director
Daisy Heath

Associate Directors
Taio Lawson & Susie McKenna

Associate Designer
Tom Piper

General Manager
Mirain Jones

New Work Associate
Tom Wright

Resident Assistant Designer
Ruth Badila

Assistant to the Artistic & Executive Director
Serena Basra

Box Office Manager
Peter Horne

Box Office Assistants
Juliet Barry, Jeremy Fowler, Lawrie MacGregor

Cleaning Supervisor
Ragne Kaldoja

Cleaners
Theresa Desmond, Karina Haro, Trish McElhill, Joslette Williamson

Head of Creative Engagement
Jenny Batt

Youth & Community Manager
Maria Shury-Smith

Schools & Pathways Manager
Juliet Styles

The Agency Project Manager
Gemma Rowan

Creative Engagement Administrator
Moni Onojeruo

Finance Director
Sophie Norvill

Finance Manager
Mick Webber

Director of Fundraising
Tessa Stanley-Price

Fundraising Manager
Catherine Walker (Maternity Leave), Ama Ofori-Darko (Maternity Cover)

Fundraising Administrator
Mishal Bandukda

Head of Marketing & Communications
Ben Prudhoe-Zdzieblo

Marketing & Communications Manager
Amy Thomas

Press Representative
Kate Morley PR

Head of Operations & Front of House
Simon Davis

Catering Manager
Angeliki Apostola

Audiences & Front of House Manager
Paul Brewster

Operations Administrator
Di Ypma

Catering & Operations Placement
James Lloyd

Duty Managers
Will Bowden, Anastasiya Kurlovich, Nieta Irons, Kal Sabir

Projectionists:
Aaron Craven-Grew, Jack Benfield, Tim Hale

IT Consultant
Richard Lucas

Head of Production
Nicki Brown

Deputy Production Manager
Scott Handley

Production & Events Technician
Dave Judd

Production Administrator
San Malhi

Board of Directors
Dawn Austwick (Chair), Nicholas Basden, Dominic Cooke CBE, Moyra Doyle, Sita McIntosh, Anneke Mendelsohn, Karen Napier, Shrina Shah, Christopher Yu

Brent Council Representatives
Cllr Muhammed Butt, Cllr Rita Conneely

CHARACTERS

JUNO
PHYSIO
CONSULTANT
SIMON
MEL
DAN
FLAT MATE
FLAT MATE'S MUM
MR. BAXTER
KEV
ELE
COUPLE
TOBY
JUSTIN

NOTES ON STAGING

JUNO, a wheelchair user, is the sole person on stage for the duration of the play.

The actress playing **JUNO** also plays all other characters and shouldn't use any props or costume to do this.

JUNO should be played by a disabled actress. If you can't find a disabled actress, then look a bit harder.

This text is part stand up, part therapy session. Hopefully the audience will leave feeling like **JUNO** is one of their best friends.

Text in italics is dialogue between characters. All other text is spoken directly to the audience. Any ellipsis indicates a beat, and should be honoured.

The majority of the play takes place in Essex.

I wouldn't worry too much about props and set – save the money for cake.

AUTHOR'S NOTE

In 2019, I sat down to write a play that explored life as a disabled woman in a way I'd never seen before. I wanted to write a character who was funny and honest and lovable and cringeworthy. A character whose disability is intrinsic to her personality, but who doesn't fall into the stereotypes we often see. A character whose experience is both unique and universal. I wanted to write about a woman like Juno. So, I set out to write a brutally honest, but (hopefully!) beautifully playful play.

When I finished that first draft, I wanted to run away and pretend it didn't exist. But then I shared a twenty-minute extract with some mates, and they encouraged me to send it off into the big wide world (thanks pals). So, off it went to The Women's Prize for Playwriting. I never thought it'd get anywhere. I just thought it'd be a good thing to say I'd done. And then it was the joint winner. Whaaaaat. It was very unexpected and a total thrill, but the main thing I kept thinking was "oh no, strangers have read my play" – it felt too personal for others to read. Too honest. I considered leaving the country, changing my name and working on a remote farm. But then I remembered that I'm allergic to most animals and I quite like my friends and family. So here I am.

This play is about love in all its forms. It is a love letter to my younger self and to all my friends and family along the way. Most of all, I hope that it's a reminder to be a little more Juno: messy, honest and joyful. I hope you like it.

And before I go… Thank you to Leigh, Hannah, Cooney, Mick, Lucy, Mel, Leo, Alexander, Alim and Stacey for all their support in the early days of this play. And thank you to everyone at The Women's Prize for Playwriting, Paines Plough, Kiln Theatre, 45North, Ellie Keel Productions, Concord and all the 'Reasons' creative team – you rock. Big thanks to my wonderful agents Lee (and everyone at Lee Morgan Management) and Mel (and everyone at Casarotto Ramsay & Associates – especially Laura).

Amy Trigg, 2021

For Mum and Dad
Thank you for everything.
Sorry about the swear words xx

Waiting Room A

JUNO. Waiting Room A.

"Elderly Medicine" looms overhead.

Around me are a dozen humans at least twenty years older than myself.

Half of us are in wheelchairs.

Everyone else is with a friend, partner or neighbour, but I am alone.

…

Welcome, my friends, to "the spina bifida day clinic".

I'm in a different room now; laying on a plastic bed.

The physio stretches my right leg.

PHYSIO. *You're very supple.*

JUNO. *Thanks, I warmed up.*

PHYSIO. *Can you move your foot towards me?*

JUNO. *Erm, no.*

PHYSIO. *Can you try?*

…

JUNO. I look at my right foot.

…

This is the moment we've all been waiting for.

I picture myself sat on the sofa with Lorraine Kelly, telling her about my medical miracle, before flying out to meet Oprah.

But nothing happens.

Next up, I head to the consultant's office.

I had a tendon transfer on it when I was younger, but it didn't work so they did a triple artho-

CONSULTANT. *Arthrodesis?*

JUNO. *Right. Bone fusion. And that worked at the time, but now it's not so "fused". It's swollen, floppy and blue. Three symptoms I recommend not googling.*

He doesn't laugh.

CONSULTANT. *The X-ray shows that it's not broken, but the tendons have weakened because of the surgery. As we get older this happens.*

JUNO. *Right, but I'm twenty three.*

CONSULTANT. *Well, it's more accelerated because of the surgery.*

...

It could well be nerve related and coming from your back. As you know we don't want to operate on that area again. We can refer you to the pain management clinic.

JUNO. *More drugs.*

CONSULTANT. *I know this isn't the answer you were hoping for.*

JUNO. *No. I'm thrilled that I spent my entire childhood having operations only for them to mean nothing now that I'm the ripe old age of twenty three.*

...

They never tell you that do they?

"Cutting your tendons and fusing your bones together is a temporary measure. We have no idea what to do

after that. Let's just hope you die before your tendons weaken too much, eh?"

Sorry, I know it's just an ankle... but for once I would like one body alteration to be worth it.

I start putting my converse on, but the pain in my ankle makes my nose go cold.

The salt water spills from my eyes, as my heart beats so fast and so loud, it might as well be in my head.

Everything is fine.

Everything's fine.

I smile at the consultant like a clown who has just been fired from the circus.

CONSULTANT. *Are you okay, Juno? Do you want a tissue?*

JUNO. *No, I'm fine.*

I race to the nearest accessible toilet and test my teleportation skills.

...

Still nothing.

I stare at myself in the mirror.

I hear the list in my head.

The list I made when I was a child.

The list that finds a way of time travelling to my present.

Everything is fine.

I return to Waiting Room A, Elderly Medicine.

The air feels dull, and the sounds seem muted.

My face is wet, but no one looks at me.

This must be what Patrick Swayze felt like before he found Whoopi Goldberg.

I consider leaving and crying into an overpriced bowl of pasta over the road at Carluccio's.

But I've still got to see the urologist and occupational therapist and...

...

...

My phone starts ringing.

It's Simon.

Simon's office is around the corner. He works at some fancy media company.

They have a free pick 'n' mix stand in the lobby. It's wild.

I answer the phone and try to sound like I haven't been crying.

Hello.

Half an hour later, Simon arrives with free pick 'n' mix.

He sits opposite me, replying to work emails on his phone.

SIMON. *Mel wants to know what time we're getting there tonight.*

JUNO. I stare intently at my jelly beans and pretend I haven't heard him.

SIMON. *Please don't make me go on my own again.*

JUNO. *You'll be fine. It's Mel and Kev.*

SIMON. *And all of Mel's work friends.*

JUNO. *I'm just not in the mood, Simon.*

...

SIMON. *Rock, paper, scissors?*

JUNO. Things just got serious.

Simon and I once ended up at Legoland on Christmas Eve because of rock, paper, scissors.

We've only known each other for a couple of years, but in that time Simon has managed to make himself irreplaceable.

He's the man who brings me sweets when I'm sad.

And forces me to drive to rainy Windsor in the middle of winter.

I know he's not really worried about going to the party on his own.

He'd be fine.

He's worried about leaving me.

Anyway, it's no longer our decision to make.

It's with the gods of fate.

We hold our hands out in fists and make solid eye contact.

JUNO/SIMON. *Three, two, one...*

Pumpkin Party

The party is at Mel and Kev's.

Recently engaged.

More recently on the rocks.

Mel greets us at the door.

MEL. *I need you two to carve the pumpkins.*

JUNO. Just to clarify… it's not a Halloween party. It's just a party with pumpkins. A pumpkin party.

Simon is given a knife because he is the responsible one.

I'm given a spoon.

I do however get entrusted with the recycling bag.

And the future of the earth is a pretty big responsibility, thank you very much.

Mel, Kev and I all went to school together.

Mel works in a posh bank, and once got sent freebies from a jewellery company to post about on Instagram.

Meanwhile, Kev once got arrested at Glastonbury whilst dressed as a cabbage.

He's a teacher.

My friends are all very grown up.

Anyway, back to me and my spoon.

JUNO. *Simon, I love you, but I just think you're an idiot.*

Simon recently broke up with Becky, and I'm one hundred percent more upset about it than he is. She was our dungeon master, and we haven't even finished our quest.

Mel storms into the room.

MEL. *Guys, disaster. I can't find the tea lights.*

SIMON. *Oh God, should we cancel the party?*

MEL. *No, Simon. Obviously not. I need you to go out and get some.*

JUNO. Mel lost her sense of humour somewhere between her move from Braintree to Brentwood. Around this time, she also lost her accent and started shopping at Waitrose.

I can ask Dan to get some on his way.

MEL. *Are you two talking again?*

JUNO. Dan and I have been on off flirting – and fornicating – since sixth form. It's all very exciting, and very dull.

Mel leaves the room with a nod and a stressed attempt at a smile.

Forty five minutes later…

DAN. *Did somebody order tea lights?*

JUNO. Dan is a bit of a douche.

But in a really attractive way.

Confidence. Arrogance. It's a fine line. And Dan straddles it like he's at a rodeo.

The party is uneventful.

Mel and Kev have muted arguments in the kitchen.

Simon cuts crudités, whilst I spoon hummus into a mosaic bowl.

I tried putting it out in the plastic tub that it comes in, but apparently we're pretending to be posh tonight.

I see Dan occasionally.

He smiles at me and I wonder if he had braces as a child or if his teeth just grew that way.

At the end of the night, we offer to help tidy up.

MEL. *No, honestly. We'll do it in the morning. Text me when you get home.*

JUNO. Mel slams the door as Kev waves at us from the kitchen.

I don't know if they're about to have sex or break up.

Maybe both.

Simon carries my wheelchair down the front steps, as I shuffle down on my bum.

I see Dan talking to a couple of Mel's work friends.

DAN. *Yeah, here, take my card.*

JUNO. He kisses me goodbye.

On the cheek.

Bit disappointing.

Simon puts my wheelchair in the boot before jumping in the passenger seat.

…

When Simon and I first met, he thought I was anti social and a "bit odd".

I thought he was an arrogant man with good bone structure who wouldn't give me the time of day.

We met at an improv class and finally got talking during our second session, when we bonded over our mutual love of Billy Joel.

…

At school I didn't really have a friend until I was fourteen.

I spent half my time at the hospital, so I couldn't offer consistency.

Or a cool reputation.

I once laughed so hard whilst drinking a Capri Sun that I got projectile snot.

My best friends were my counsellors.

I don't like to brag but... I had two.

I guess that's what happens when you try and throw yourself out of a window aged eight.

...

I pull into Simon's driveway but instead of getting out, he stays put...

SIMON. *You gonna go straight home?*

JUNO. *Yep.*

SIMON. *No detours?*

JUNO. *Nope.*

SIMON. *You're wearing matching underwear, aren't you?*

JUNO. *Okay, firstly that's a really weird thing to ask and secondly, it doesn't mean anything.*

SIMON. *It means everything.*

JUNO. *Oh my God, Simon!*

Once he disappears into the darkness of his much-nicer-than-my-flat-flat, I pull out my mobile...

JUNO TEXT. *Hey, didn't get to talk to you much tonight. Want to grab a drink... question mark, send.*

DAN TEXT. *Sure, where?*

...

JUNO TEXT. *McDonalds... question mark, send.*

...

It's twenty four hour.

...

DAN TEXT. *Want to come back to mine?*

JUNO. Yes, please, god. Absolutely.

Dan and his Seahorse

JUNO. Half an hour later, I'm sat in his bedroom.

Dan's flatmate is next door.

The walls are thin and he's FaceTiming his mum.

FLATMATE. *Do you have a rough time?*

FLATEMATE'S MUM. *Oh, I don't know dear. You know what traffic can be like on a Sunday.*

FLATMATE. *You'll need to park in Clarence Street.*

FLATEMATE'S MUM. *Ooh, have you moved?*

FLATMATE. *No. It's the road behind ours –*

FLATEMATE'S MUM. *Well, we'll just park on your driveway.*

FLATEMATE. *I told you. There are road closures so –*

FLATEMATE'S MUM. *There are what?*

FLATEMATE. *There are road closures.*

FLATEMATE'S MUM. *Say it again.*

FLATEMATE. *Road. Closures.*

FLATEMATE'S MUM. *Oh, hang on, you've frozen.*

    (Calling into another room.)

  Charlie?

JUNO. ...

We've not kissed yet.

We're watching Futurama.

Is that a new lamp?

DAN. Yeah.

JUNO. *Is it a... seahorse?*

DAN. *Yeah, I just like seahorses. I prefer them over starfish.*

JUNO. ...

DAN. *Do you want some brioche?*

JUNO. ...

Yeah, okay then.

...

He's different in private.

Less of a douche.

He never holds my hand.

Which is okay.

I don't like my hands.

They're rough because of my eczema.

And the wheeling.

We talk for what feels like two weeks.

Or rather he talks, and I impatiently nod and smile.

And then... we begin.

The first time I took my clothes off in front of Dan, I warned him about my scars.

He told me that he didn't care.

Which was nice of him.

I turn off the seahorse as he reaches for a condom.

I ask if it's latex free.

It isn't.

Which is a bit frustrating because we've been through this.

each for my own.

People with spina bifida are more likely to have latex allergies.

Which is really something we should learn about in sex ed.

MR. BAXTER. *Yes, well we don't have any disabled students.*

JUNO. *Well, Mr. Baxter what about when one of your students has a disabled sexual partner?*

MR. BAXTER. *Don't be ridiculous!*

JUNO. Long story short: I was not part of the sex ed story.

For a long time, I didn't know how it'd work.

Or what I'd be able to feel.

People would ask me if I could have sex and I'd feign shock and act wildly offended, whilst secretly wanting to grab them by the shoulders and be like: "I don't know, Janet!"

Every time the opportunity arose.

I'd make an excuse.

I told my first – and only – boyfriend that I was Catholic and saving myself.

He got me a promise ring and told me he'd wait, and I immediately broke up with him.

So, I guess I'll be going to hell.

Eventually, I discovered google.

It was a bit like reading the iMDB parental guide before watching a horror film.

But instead of reading about violence, profanity and frightening scenes, I'd read about sensation, positions and lube.

With this newfound knowledge, I decided that I wanted to get it over and done with.

And done, I did get.

It was with this guy, let's call him Dan, because shock horror, it was in fact seahorse Dan.

And now here we are.

Four years down the line.

With a guy who would be happy for me to have an allergic reaction in my vagina.

Call me crazy, friends, but I don't think I'm going to marry Dan.

He's made little attempt to understand my body.

He still tries positions that are very ambitious for your average Joanne, let alone a Joanne who has next to no control over her lower limbs.

I try to tell him when something won't work, but he sees it as a challenge, rather than an uncomfortable impossibility.

I can't feel everything, which would probably be fine if I was being stimulated in other ways, but I'm currently tuning back into the conversation next door and hearing about Dan's flatmate's issues with his mum's new boyfriend, Charlie, so I would say that I'm not quite as excited as I should be.

Dan seems happy.

So, that's good, eh?

Afterwards – yeah, it's over – Dan puts his arms around me and begins to snore.

He looks softer when he's asleep.

I look at my phone.

Four forty seven.

I google what time McDonalds starts serving breakfast.

Five.

Dan. Dan. Dan?

DAN. *Hmm?*

JUNO. *I'm gonna go.*

DAN. *Okay. Bye.*

...

JUNO. *Right, bye.*

After our passionate farewell I put my clothes on, quietly.

I get to his front door and sit on the doorstep, quietly.

There are five large concrete steps at his front door.

He has always helped me in.

But going out I've always done alone.

It takes me a few minutes.

I'm trying to do it very... quietly.

It's been raining so my bum is wet.

I'm wetter now than I was half an hour ago.

Not ideal.

I know Dan isn't exactly Prince Charming.

But at least I know what I'm getting.

And maybe more importantly he knows what he's getting...

And also, it's just nice that someone wants to... you know...

It's a good set up.

...

Attack of the Appendix

(We find ourselves in a painfully white hospital room.)

JUNO. Something has gone wrong.

It feels like I'm being stabbed from the inside.

…

When I was six, my parents noticed that I wasn't developing properly.

We already knew that I had spina bifida.

We learned that fun fact at birth.

But at six, things weren't quite going according to plan.

So, I was sent for my first MRI scan.

Put that in your baby book and smoke it.

Later, I'd develop a fear of MRI's, so my parents built a cardboard version for me at home.

It was covered in tin foil, and collapsible – so actually very practical.

It was like if Neil Buchanan built a horizontal space ship.

I'd lay in it and get used to existing in an enclosed space.

A safe space.

Mum and dad would make loud noises from the outside.

It was basically immersive theatre.

Or the initiation into a low-key cult.

er that first MRI, the consultant called my parents
a side room.

They wanted to take me straight into surgery.

...

I used to imagine my parents' reaction of shock horror.

But now I imagine that they stayed silent and still for a long time.

Listening, as the man in front of them said words they barely understood.

Later that day, my surgeon spent hours de tethering my spinal cord, by releasing nerves and removing fat and bone.

I spent weeks in hospital recovering.

It was one of the best holidays I can remember.

Because I don't remember the pain or the physio or the needles.

I remember the Halloween party.

And the nurses.

And the movie nights.

And I remember my mum and dad making notes whenever a doctor came round.

And Dad staying in a nearby hotel.

And Mum making me toast in the ward kitchen.

My parents were my best friends growing up.

Even when I blamed them for everything and said things that I can never take back.

They made sure that I was never alone.

And when my world became dark, and I grew fed up with the pain and the fuss and the longevity of it all; they got me help.

And when I latched onto things that I loved, they did everything in their power to make sure that those things were ever present in my life.

Which is why we saw the musical *Cats* seventeen times.

I did everything with my parents.

And I loved it.

But it meant that I led a very sheltered life.

I'm trying really hard to do things on my own.

But when I'm back in a hospital room, unsure of what's happening... they are the people that I want by my side.

...

Simon returns with a coffee and a KitKat.

SIMON. *So, could you still get appendicitis?*

JUNO. *No. Apparently not.*

It's technically my appendix that's bleeding.

When I was thirteen, I was fitted up with an ACE stoma.

My appendix was used to create a tunnel from the surface of my stomach to my large intestine.

There's no bag involved, just a hole covered with a plaster.

I'm reassured that it's still the best option.

But right now, it doesn't feel like it.

Simon didn't know about any of this until one o'clock this afternoon.

I typically choose not to tell my friends about my appendix and its many uses.

orry that they'll see me in a different light, or that
r appendixes will feel inferior.

Simon's spent the last couple of hours googling the procedure and informing me on the latest medical gossip surrounding bowel management.

If I didn't love him, I'd want to punch him in the throat.

SIMON. *So, what happens if you get pregnant? Does the hole get massive?*

JUNO. *I don't know, Simon.*

SIMON. *Makes you wonder how elastic your appendix is, doesn't it?*

JUNO. *Does it?*

SIMON. *Can you get pregnant?*

JUNO. ...

I'm caught off guard.

It's a question that I'm used to.

From strangers.

Not from my friends.

Yes. Technically. Well, loads of people with spina bifida have kids but everyone is different.

SIMON. *Do you want kids?*

JUNO. ...

I don't know.

Do you?

SIMON. *Yeah. Three, I think.*

...

JUNO. The doctor returns holding a few freshly printed sheets of paper.

He hasn't heard of the ACE.

Not many people have.

Sometimes I wonder if my old surgeon just fancied trying something new out on my intestine.

A designer stoma. Limited edition.

Simon and the doctor compare web pages, and an hour later we're allowed to leave.

My stoma area isn't infected, but it's inflamed.

They've put a special small tube in the hole to keep it open until the inflammation dies down.

It means that I can't bend over, and it hurts to laugh.

Simon makes me laugh the entire journey home.

It is agony.

But lovely.

We get home and raid my half-eaten advent calendar.

And I call my parents.

The Wedding

(We are transported via bright lights and cheesy music to our next location...)

JUNO. The wedding of the century comes round sooner than expected.

Mel is in a white dress.

MEL. *I could literally get an annulment right now.*

JUNO. She's angry, but she looks sensational.

MEL. *We haven't even cut the bloody cake!*

JUNO. We're in the accessible bathroom of a barn in the middle of North Essex.

Simon has just stuck his fingers down the groom's throat.

We cheer when Kev throws up like he's a baby who's just burped for the first time.

Kev tipped from tipsy to drunk just before the first dance.

We watched helplessly as Kev gyrated against Mel in front of their entire extended family.

MEL. *Simon, did you let him have shots?*

JUNO. Simon isn't the best man.

The best man is Kev's cousin.

A man who once ended up in A&E with a burned arsehole.

Simon, in his role as groomsman, is responsible for both of them.

Mel is called to the bar by her mum.

Kev watches her leave, like a retriever being left at the kennels for a long weekend.

KEV. *I just love her, Simon. She looks like Princess Jasmine!*

JUNO. The last time I saw him this drunk was at our year thirteen leavers prom.

We'd spent the night being the poster kids for our sixth form.

I'm disabled, Kev is Black, and Mel is mixed race.

When Mel came out as bi in year twelve, it was like an early Christmas present for our head of year.

After an exhausting night of smiling and pretending not to know why we were always chosen for the newspaper photographs, we headed to Kev's house.

His parents, for some unknown reason, decided it'd be a good idea to go away for the night, and leave us to throw a house party.

They were worried about Kev not making friends.

He joined us half way through year twelve, when he moved from Dagenham.

Which made him a minor celebrity.

At the party I slept in the surprisingly spacious spare room, and woke up in the morning to the smell of burning flesh.

I looked down.

My foot was red, white and... melting.

I called Kev in from the bathroom, where he was brushing his teeth.

He saw my foot and immediately gagged on his Colgate.

I'd slept with my foot up against the radiator.

Apparently, it was on...

Eventually I got a skin graft.

But first I spent months visiting the burns unit every day to get it dressed.

Luckily, I couldn't feel a thing.

Ahh, nerve damage.

I was offered morphine and other high-end drugs, but I never had anything. Not even a paracetamol.

Basically, I saved the NHS a lot of money and they're welcome.

Kev came with me to get my dressing changed once.

My foot was red and the toe nail was black.

When they pulled away the gauze, Kev fainted and I had to call his dad to pick him up from the burns unit.

...

Back in the accessible bathroom, Kev throws up again.

KEV. *Thank you for being here.*

JUNO. Kev looks like he's been dragged through a hedge.

Simon still looks photo ready which is annoying.

Mate, if you want to get back to Lucy then I'll be fine with Kev.

Lucy is Simon's latest girlfriend. I've only met her a few times, but she's already told me that her cousin is disabled so she knows exactly what I've been through.

Simon doesn't leave.

We share a half-eaten French stick whilst listening to *Come on Eileen* play from the hall next door.

It's bliss.

But after two more songs, I return Kev to Mel.

And Simon to Lucy.

And I wonder if I'd like someone to return to.

...

Healing is a Devised Project

JUNO. Mel and Kev show me their honeymoon photos, before Mel demands that I tell her everything she missed whilst she was away.

MEL. *How religious is he?*

JUNO. *Pretty religious.*

I've been invited to a Christian rock concert tonight, by my cousin's flatmate, Toby.

Mel is adamant that I've been asked out on a date.

But I haven't.

I don't think.

Oh God.

…

Mel once played Jesus in our school production of *Jesus Christ Superstar*.

I was enthusiastic ensemble.

At one point the entire cast went to Jesus Mel to be healed.

Boys pretending to be blind, threw down their canes and kissed Mel's feet.

Girls chucked their crutches and walking sticks into the wings before an elaborate dance break.

Our teacher suggested that I left the stage at that point.

…

Months later Mel and I were on our way home from school when a group of humans stopped us.

I'm still not sure which church they were a part of, but they were very nice.

They offered to heal me.

And I wasn't in a rush, so I was like "sure!"

Suddenly there were hands, very respectfully, placed on my body.

They started mumbling, then chanting and then speaking in unison.

I tried to guess whether they rehearsed with a script or if it was more of a devised project.

A few minutes later, I was told by a younger man in the group to get up and walk.

...

Bit of background: I could walk a little bit when I was younger. It actually wasn't until I was eight that I started using a wheelchair, and it was a few years after that when walking became a total thing of the past.

So, when I was sat in that car park being healed by strangers, I was wearing leg splints and could still manage a few steps.

The question is: should I have gone into more detail about my diagnosis before the prayer session?

Not one to disappoint, I stood and stumbled a few metres across the car park, before returning to my chair.

My new friends cheered and applauded.

And I tried to explain about my splints, but it was no good.

It'd gone too far.

They all shook my hand and I thanked them and took a leaflet for their church.

...

After they'd gone, Mel turned to me

MEL. *So, are you going to walk home then?*

...

JUNO. The Christian rock concert is actually pretty good.

I sit in the corner, sipping my lime and soda whilst watching Toby play bass.

He's very talented.

After his set, he introduces me to his friends.

ELE. *Toby says you're coming to Sunday service?*

JUNO. *Yeah, I'm looking forward to it.*

And I actually am.

...

A couple in their forties approach us.

The others greet them enthusiastically.

I guess that they're the Kardashians of the Christian world.

Toby introduces me and they seem to know who I am.

I still have no idea whether this is a date or not but I'm starting to realise that Toby reminds me a bit of Paul Rudd and I'm wondering if he'd be interested in dressing up as Ant Man when I notice the Kardashian couple have asked me a question.

Pardon?

COUPLE. *May we pray for you?*

JUNO:

...

I'm reminded that I'm broken.

I look at Toby and his friends.

They look... like they're at church.

...

Yeah, sure. Thanks.

I brace myself for hands to be placed on my body, but nothing happens.

Apparently, this prayer take place at a distance.

The others soon leave, and Toby and I are left alone.

I realise that it's not a date.

...

Do you think God loves me?

...

TOBY. *Yes, of course he does.*

JUNO. *Then why did he make me this way?*

TOBY. *God only sends us the challenges that we can cope with.*

JUNO. *I was once told that it's because I'd sinned in a previous life.*

TOBY. *It's perhaps a sign of the original sin. Not necessarily yours.*

...

Disabilities aren't permanent. "We await a Saviour, the Lord Jesus Christ, who will transform our lowly body to be like His glorious body."

...

I think God could really help you. He loves you.

...

JUNO. *Well, I don't know about you, but I'm getting very mixed signals.*

We're told that all of God's creatures are perfect, but that's not true, is it? Because if I was perfect then why would people need to pray for me?

And I know people don't want me to be in pain and I appreciate that, and so many people are so kind. But whenever someone prays for me... they never ask what I want the prayer to be about. They just pray that one day I will be able to walk. Across the car park or down the aisle or whatever.

If I was to pray for something – or wish for something – then being able to walk wouldn't be top of my list. It's maybe on the list but it's not the top priority.

...

Every time someone offers to pray for me... or heal me... I feel a little bit further away from perfect. I feel like I'm an unfinished project. And it's my job to break it to people that I'm never going to be finished.

...

...

I look at Toby.

I feel like I'm in therapy.

Or at church.

I consider telling him about the list but...

...

He walks me to my car, and we say goodbye.

Just as I'm about to close the door, he stops me.

TOBY. *I'm not going to pray for you.*

JUNO. I see the rebellious glint in his eyes.

But then I see the guilt flash across his face in the same second.

And we say goodbye for the second time.

New Year's Eve

JUNO. We celebrate New Year's Eve at Simon's flat

At the front of his building is a makeshift ramp, painted like the yellow brick road.

Simon first painted it for Halloween, when we all dressed up as characters from *The Wizard of Oz* – except for Kev who insisted on coming as an oxo cube.

KEV. *Well, I like gravy, don't I?*

JUNO. I see Dan.

It's been a while.

He smiles at me the way he always has.

But I notice that he smiles at a lot of people that way.

He corners me in the hallway.

DAN. *Yeah, Heather, I've been seeing her for a few months now. She plays squash.*

JUNO. I knew I wouldn't be heart broken when Dan started seeing someone.

But I didn't think I'd feel nothing.

Mel spends the majority of the evening avoiding our old school friends.

Maybe she'd like to avoid me.

...

Kev is drunk and sat on my lap for the countdown.

He hugs me so tight that I can hardly breathe.

Fireworks go off in the distance, as Mel hands round lyric sheets for *Auld Lang Syne*.

At two a.m., once most people have left, we realise that we haven't used the sparklers.

Kev grabs six and lights them all at once.

KEV. *I'm the Firestarter...*

MEL. *Kev. Stop it. You're too close. Kev. Stop it! I'm wearing cashmere.*

...

When I was fifteen, Mel and I spent New Year's at a bus stop.

We were on our way to a party, but didn't get there in time.

We eventually arrived at twelve thirty six.

Justin Rogers opened the door to his parents' semi detached.

Now, I'm not saying that Justin Rogers was the most beautiful human on the planet.

But Justin Rogers was the most beautiful human on the planet.

Still is.

Anyway, I'd had a minor crush on Justin ever since the first day of secondary school.

When I say "minor" I mean...

I'd memorise his school timetable and make sure that I was outside the correct classroom at all times.

He once broke both of his arms and had to leave class five minutes early to beat the rush of people.

I also left early, because of my wheelchair.

This meant five minutes alone time in the empty corridors of the science block with Justin Rogers, every Tuesday and Thursday morning.

I was thrilled.

When his arms healed, I considered hiring a hit man in year eleven to take out his ankles.

Did I mention that I had a pillowcase with his face on it? Because I did.

Are you starting to see that I had issues? Because I did.

Justin pointed out the bathroom for Mel, before leading me into the dimly lit conservatory.

The music had been turned down, because of the neighbours, so I could hear my classmates chatting and laughing in the lounge next door.

Justin sat on the wicker sofa.

I placed myself a full six feet away and put my hands on my hips, inspecting the newly built extension like an enthusiastic estate agent.

Word on the street was that Justin was "interested" in me.

This was maddeningly exciting, but it also made me feel like a car waiting to be taken out on a test drive.

I'd never kissed anyone at this point, so I was fresh off the forecourt.

I commented on the lovely alcove before Justin finally spoke.

JUSTIN. *Did you kiss anyone at midnight?*

JUNO. *I was in a bus stop with Mel so, no.*

JUSTIN. *Did you want one?*

JUNO. *What?*

JUSTIN. *A kiss.*

JUNO. *What from Mel? Nah, I'm alright.*

JUSTIN. *I didn't get one.*

JUNO. *Oh, that's a shame.*

JUSTIN. *I'm asking if I can kiss you.*

JUNO. *Oh.*

...

JUSTIN. *Don't worry. Forget I said anything.*

JUNO. *No, I um – just – well – I um – have – I would – god erm – hmm – argh.*

JUSTIN. *You're just making noises.*

JUNO. *I would like to. It's just that you're there and I'm here and they're in there and... and... it's hot innit?*

...

JUSTIN. *Right, I'm gonna kiss you now.*

JUNO. And he did.

...

And there were no fireworks.

There was no swell of music.

But... there was a very noticeable change in altitude.

He pulled away.

And I opened my eyes.

...

And there was... silence.

...

And I thought...

Wait. This doesn't make sense.

Why would Justin Rogers want to kiss me?

Because it's not just a kiss, is it?

Kissing is a tool.

A tool to sniff out the perfect mate in order to survive.

Now, this concerns me, because from an animalistic point of view, I might not be the best genetic partner.

Forget about the not fully-formed spine.

We're talking allergies, eczema, bouts of depression, a terrible taste in music –

Kissing leads to love, and love means seeing a future.

With someone.

And why would someone choose to deal with all the shit that I have to deal with?

From a scientific and evolutionary point of view...

It doesn't make sense.

Justin Rogers looked at me.

And I looked back.

But all I thought about was... the list.

...

I help Simon pick up burnt-out sparklers.

His latest girlfriend, Stacey, was meant to be here.

But apparently, they're no longer seeing each other.

Simon, do you actually want to be in a relationship?

SIMON. *Yeah, of course I do.*

JUNO. *But you never let anything grow. Mate, I need a spreadsheet to keep track of your love life.*

He looks at me like I'm his mum who's just told him to tidy his room.

...

The truth is I like it when Simon is single.

I think about what will happen when he meets someone and settles down.

I'll be happy for him.

But I'll be left behind.

He'll be Andy and I'll be Woody.

Fortunately, he seems incapable of forming lasting romantic relationships.

So, I think we're good.

I'm often asked if Simon and I are a couple.

People assume that I must have hidden feelings for him.

The thing is, they're not hidden.

I platonically love him with all my heart.

And maybe that's enough for me.

Standby

JUNO. I step away from people for a few weeks.

My doctors and I are experimenting with different drugs.

Some days are better than others.

Mostly I'm tired.

But I can't sleep.

So, I'm really fun to be around.

It's four a.m. and the pain has stopped, so I know I'll be able to sleep soon.

Just not quite yet.

I call these weeks my "standby weeks".

I shut off from everything I can.

I don't talk on the phone.

I don't go out.

I eat well, go to work, and focus on giving my body time.

I learnt to look after my body at quite a young age.

I stopped drinking when I was twenty because I realised that I already had very little control over my body, and I didn't want to lose any more.

Whenever people ask me why I don't drink, I just say I had a couple of bad experiences.

And I did. I'm not lying.

But I never mention the one bad experience that tipped me firmly over to sobriety.

Never.

…

It was September, twenty twelve.

The sun was shining, and the Paralympics had given me a god like position in society.

Kev was having a beer and pizza night with some old school friends, and this boy who I'd liked for about nine years was there.

Let's call him Justin Rogers. Remember him?

Shortly after our first kiss at his New Year's Eve party, I had discovered alcohol.

Drunk Juno would make out with Justin at every possible party.

Sober Juno would awkwardly avoid Justin by any means necessary.

This seemed to suit us both.

And really helped cement my fear of commitment.

We hadn't seen each other in over a year, but I'd decided that tonight was the night.

I was going to fulfil the nine-year prophecy, and finally sleep with Justin Rogers.

I was fully prepared. I was also fully drunk and getting drunkerer.

At eleven o five I decided to kiss him.

He was half way through exhaling smoke from his cigarette and I thought, yeah now seems like a good time.

In my drunken haste to shove my tongue down his throat, I knocked his drink over.

So, there he was... wet and choking.

Just like I'd planned.

We went upstairs to get him some dry clothes.

He carried me, because I couldn't walk.

I couldn't walk anyway but trust me that night I really couldn't walk.

He was holding me like he was Kevin Costner, and as I looked into his eyes, I knew this was it.

I was his Whitney.

This was the moment.

Our moment.

Nine years in the making.

Be still my beating heart.

He opened his mouth...

JUSTIN. *What's that?*

...

Are you...?

...

JUNO. It took me a second too long to realise that at the very moment I was planning my wedding to Justin Rogers, my bladder had decided to betray me.

Let's be fair, it wasn't her fault.

She's neurogenic and full of vodka.

It was never going to end well.

I considered my situation.

Surely everyone's pissed on someone, right?

This was something we'd laugh about at our wedding, right?

It'd be our thing, right?

Right?

I saw no other option.

I rolled myself out of his arms and flopped down the stairs one by one.

Flopping down a set of stairs whilst catastrophically drunk feels a bit like being on a slow motion rollercoaster.

I felt my stomach turn over and heard Justin shout from the upstairs landing, as I grabbed the shoe box by the front door, and threw up a red mix of vodka, Domino's and regret.

Justin and I never spoke again.

Which really cemented my fear of intimacy.

Shortly after the vodka induced bladder betrayal of twenty twelve, I gave up drinking.

And I haven't pissed on a guy since.

But never say never.

What's Wrong With Me...?

JUNO. It takes two more weeks and several changes in medication but finally I'm back to a normal sleeping pattern.

My social life gets switched back on and KAPOW.

She's back bitches.

Did you miss me?

On Monday, I see my parents.

My brother, Elliot and his husband Luke are visiting from Edinburgh.

Luke grew up in Scotland but doesn't have a Scottish accent.

He also works for the government.

So, I'm pretty sure he's a spy.

On Wednesday, Simon and I watch Kev play hockey.

Mel doesn't make it because of work.

The hall is freezing.

We sit huddled together drinking cold sugary tea and go for a kebab afterwards.

I watch Simon cut up his chips.

He uses a knife and fork for everything.

Even pizza.

It's at this kebab place that Simon and I decide to finally join the rest of our generation, and download a dating app.

I thought Simon was already on them but apparently, he just meets women at bars.

He is that attractive.

I'm glad I didn't know Simon when I was younger.

I think he might've been a bit too cool for me.

When I first met his mum, she showed me "embarrassing" photos of him as a child.

He looked like the spawn of Harry Styles and Beyonce.

Meanwhile, I looked like a cross between Shirley Temple and Chuckie from Rugrats.

Not that I really cared about what I looked like when I was little.

Never really registered that kind of thing.

Not till later.

...

I grew up in a cul-de-sac.

My brother and I would go and knock for our friends and we'd have water fights or play run outs or compete in overly-competitive-soon-to-be-banned conker fights.

I was too busy to care about what I looked like.

Then one day, one of the cul-de-sac boys suggested we play kiss chase.

I must stress that this boy was, like... nine? Imagine being that confident at nine.

Anyway, I remember thinking that I didn't really like any of the boys in my road but hey, I could go for a kiss.

We started playing, even though I don't think anyone understood the rules. It was basically one boy running around trying to kiss someone and then if he "caught" someone, they also became a kisser. Like germ transferring vampires.

If there was a soundtrack to "Cul-De-Sac Kiss Chase" it'd be the Sex and the City theme tune played on a kazoo.

The other girls started screaming and running away and I quickly followed suit, giggling and limping towards the shelter of the conker tree.

My splints slowed me down, which would normally be a bad thing in sports, but this was kiss chase... surely losing was the point, right?

As I slowly hobbled away, I became aware of one thing...

I was not being chased.

I looked back, checking that everyone knew I was still alive.

By this point there were several kissers and only one or two kids yet to be caught.

I started limping in slow circles. I was practically serving myself on a dish to these boys and what did they do?

RUN TO THE GIRLS WHO HAD ALREADY BEEN KISSED.

And then I realised...

No one wanted to kiss me.

I began shuffling away, past the conker trees and towards my house.

The soundtrack had changed. It was now Bridget Jones on a violin.

Red and blotchy, I sat and cried to my mum about how no one wanted to kiss me, how no one liked me and how much I hated myself. My mum cuddled me and told me it was going to be okay.

I sat and watched Recess for a few hours, before there was a knock on the door.

All the cul-de-sac kids were stood on our driveway, holding signs: "Kisses for Juno" or "We love Juno".

I giggled because if I didn't giggle, I was going to cry.

I didn't want to go out.

And I didn't want to be kissed.

I felt special in all the wrong ways.

Everyone gave me a quick peck on the cheek and then someone wanted to play hide and seek so I went and hid in my room.

That night, as I sat down to smiley faces, beans and sausages, I prayed that this was never spoken about again.

And it wasn't.

…

And now kiss chase has been replaced with apps.

Great.

To no one's surprise, Simon immediately plans a date with a girl from Tinder.

She's a Canadian woman living in Bromley by the name of Sophie.

She's six years younger than him and doesn't know who Kim Possible is.

I give it a week.

My success is not so immediate, but after a few days we start getting some bites…

I sit at my desk and coyly open a message from a new match.

"I'm going to fuck you so hard you can walk"

Bit forward.

Other first messages I've received include...

"You're too pretty to be in a wheelchair."

"What happened?"

"You're really inspiring."

"What's wrong with you?"

Since I find myself with a lot of free time, I decide to answer these messages in heavy detail...

Hi Jeff, nice to meet you.

In answer to your question: I have spina bifida.

Spina bifida means "split spine" in Latin.

Ooh, fancy.

Basically, the spine doesn't develop properly whilst in the womb.

Most spina bifida cases can be detected at the twenty-week scan.

Which is around the same time you can find out the baby's sex.

And yet, I have never been invited to a spina bifida reveal party.

They didn't pick up on my spina bifida before birth, which is a bit wild because I have a lump at the base of my spine which as a baby was large enough to balance a teacup on.

There are three main types of spina bifida:

Myelomeningocele, which is the most severe type.

Meningocele, which is less severe but still pretty intense.

And then spina bifida occulta, which is the most common and the most chill of all the different types. Sometimes people don't even get diagnosed until they're into adulthood. At which point they can only join the ranks if recommended by a fully fledged member.

There is a massive array of symptoms when it comes to spina bifida and every single person is different.

It's like a buffet.

But someone else is choosing what goes on your plate.

Don't like brie?

Too bad, here's a plate full.

Some of the most common symptoms are:

– Paralysis.

– Incontinence.

– Weakness in the lower body.

– Loss of sensation.

– And latex allergies.

Something for everyone!

I can't imagine life without spina bifida.

Life would be unrecognisable.

I would be... unrecognisable.

...

Look Jeff, I can work out from our initial exchange – and your questionable topless photo with a sedated tiger – that we might not be the perfect match.

So, before I leave you and delete my profile forever, I'd just like to refer back to your initial statement: "I'm going to fuck you so hard you can walk."

Now, the fact that you think your penis has the ability to enable me to walk is both heart warming and terrifying.

That is one "big" responsibility.

If you have the power to heal someone by having sex with them, then I can only imagine that you're in high demand.

So, please ensure that you continue with your visits to the STD clinic, and remember...

With great power, comes great responsibility.

Come responsibly.

Have we checked in on Mel?

(JUNO and MEL are sat in a car wash.)

JUNO. The first thing I did after passing my driving test was pick Mel up and head to the car wash.

We played *Busted*, and sung at the top of our lungs whilst eating Jammie Dodgers.

It became our thing, and every now and then we still grab some food, go to the local garage, and have a catch up.

Today is particularly special because it's been a while and...

I brought sushi.

I didn't eat sushi for a long time because I thought it was posh food.

It's actually just rice and cucumber and shit.

I bloody love it.

I tell Mel about Simon's latest dating news.

His tinder girlfriend, Sophie, is back in Toronto, and they're trying to make the long distance thing work, which is laughable because Simon can barely make the short distance thing work.

I realise that Mel is barely listening.

She keeps looking at her phone.

She tells me about work.

She talks about it for a long time.

She's telling me about this client, who specifically requested her, when she stops talking and looks down.

Are you okay mate?

MEL. *Why am I not happy?*

...

I'm not happy. And I should be. I have a good job. I have Kev. I have my house. But – I've been offered a promotion. And I don't think I want it. Am I ungrateful?

JUNO. *No, you're not. You're not ungrateful.*

MEL. *I'm a horrible person.*

JUNO. *No, you're not.*

MEL. *Why aren't you listening to me? I'm a horrible person. Everyone would be happier without me because I'm not fun anymore. Kev's going to leave me. And you hate me. Simon is only friends with me because of you and Kev, so I won't have him. All I'll have is Kirsty and Bryan from work, who told me to get Invisalign and cut my hair. And I'm fat!*

JUNO. *You're not fat Mel. And even if you were. It's just fat.*

MEL. *So, you think I should get Invisalign?*

JUNO. *Do you want Invisalign?*

MEL. *No! I wish I was more like you. You don't care what you look like.*

JUNO. *Does Kev know how you're feeling?*

MEL. *No! I can't lose him. You don't understand. You don't know what it is because you've never been there. You can't deal with any form of intimacy; you can't even hold someone's hand, so do not tell me how to behave with my husband.*

JUNO. It feels like a punch in the gut.

So, you're not happy at work?

MEL. *No! It's so stressful. I have no idea what I'm doing with my life.*

JUNO. I go to hug her.

MEL. *Don't touch me. You weren't there when I needed you. You haven't bothered with me for weeks and now you're here. Why are you here?*

JUNO. *I'm sorry. I was on standby for a bit –*

MEL. *Adults don't get to go on standby. Just grow up!*

...

It's not fair. How are you so happy all the time?

JUNO. *I'm not.*

MEL. *Yes, you are.*

JUNO. *I thought you were happy.*

MEL. *I'm not.*

JUNO. *Well, here we are then.*

...

I think about divorce rates, as water washes over the windscreen.

...

I look at my best friend.

And I know we have work to do.

We've been giving each other the Instagram treatment.

She knows very little about my life.

And apparently, I know very little about hers.

Mel stops crying.

MEL. *I'd quite like a hug now if that's okay?*

JUNO. We hold each other for a few minutes.

It's longer than we've ever hugged.

I want to tell her that I cry too.

I want to tell her about all the times I've wanted a hug.

I want to tell her about the list.

But I don't.

…

The following Monday, Mel refuses the promotion at work.

A few weeks later, she starts her Invisalign treatment.

She doesn't cut her hair.

She starts to take actual lunch breaks at work, and she goes to the doctors and they give her some tablets.

Mel is fragile.

But she lets other people know that she's fragile.

And that seems to make her a little bit stronger.

…

I realise how insecure my beautiful friend is about the way she looks.

And I want to scream.

At first, I take it very personally.

This wonderful, smart woman has a fully functioning body.

She doesn't have a single scar.

She is fit and healthy.

And she isn't happy.

…

She starts a weight loss and fitness programme.

Months go by, and I watch as she posts "before and after photos."

Her "before photos" are what most people can only dream of.

I think about my own body.

Does she think I'm repulsive?

We've been in changing rooms together.

Has she looked at my scarred back, and toneless tummy and wasting purple legs and been repulsed?

If a woman like her can be so unhappy with her body...

Then how am I meant to feel?

Because on paper, I'm deformed.

...

But then it's a vicious cycle, isn't it?

Because I'm sure there are loads of people who would think I'm a dick for complaining about parts of my body that they would be overjoyed to have.

I know that we can't turn that voice off.

And I'm not angry with Mel.

I'm angry with everything that's made us think this way.

For a while I've had this feeling that Mel didn't like me as much as she once did.

But actually, she didn't like herself.

And I missed it.

I missed it.

...

See Ya Woody

JUNO. Kev stops playing hockey for a bit.

He concentrates on Mel.

I call her every day.

Some days she wants to talk.

Other days she doesn't.

But I still call.

Simon is still doing the whole long distance thing with Sophie, which is apparently very time consuming.

And a bit pointless.

We meet for breakfast one Sunday morning

Simon takes a sip of his coffee and tries to pretend that what he's just told me is the most normal thing in the world.

...

When did you apply for the transfer?

SIMON. *About a month ago.*

JUNO. *Do Mel and Kev know?*

SIMON. *Yeah.*

JUNO. *I'm the last to know?*

SIMON. *Yeah.*

...

JUNO. *When do you leave?*

SIMON. *Erm, I've got another four weeks.*

JUNO. *Okay.*

...

...

SIMON. *She's the best person I've ever met.*

JUNO. *Oh, well that's good.*

...

It just feels a bit quick. You're moving halfway across the world with someone you've known for what? A few months.

SIMON. *It's my longest relationship.*

JUNO. *Not exactly hard, Simon. You go through girls like you go through Pringles.*

...

Obviously, it's great and exciting and... I mean it's fine. I can still see you. I can visit you and you'll be coming home for Christmas and stuff, won't you?

SIMON. ...

...

JUNO. *I'm really gonna miss you.*

SIMON. *I'll miss you too, mate.*

...

JUNO. Simon has always felt like a lifebuoy.

Like my parents did when I was younger.

Like they still do.

But Simon is leaving.

I want to grab onto him and never let him go.

I want to be able stare at his face whenever I like.

And get annoyed with him when he tells me how to cook pasta.

A month later, and the best person I've ever met leaves.

I've never experienced heartache before.

I thought it'd feel like a broken heart.

But it feels more stretched than broken.

Like my heart is in Toronto but it's also in Essex, and in every place inbetween.

It feels like a very elastic pancake.

It's painful.

…

Mel and I start up our weekly car wash dates again.

But we don't listen to music.

I sign up to an improv class.

But I don't go in.

Because what if they don't like me?

The End of the Prequel

The list is back.

During a particularly bad panic attack, I call my parents.

They arrive and take me back to theirs.

Every night is awful because I'm terrified that it'll happen again.

But Mum climbs into bed with me, and strokes my hair until I sleep.

Everything is fine.

Every morning, Dad makes me a smoothie and delivers it to me like I'm at a spa.

He orders those little cocktail umbrellas to really complete the experience.

Everything is fine.

And yet...

I want to crawl into a small dark space and never return.

...

...

When I was eight, I tried to throw myself out of a window.

I don't think I tried very hard.

But I tried.

...

I was eight.

...

I'd made a list. Two lists.

On one piece of paper, I wrote all the things I loved about myself

And on the other I wrote all the things I hated.

I decided that if the hate list spilled over onto another page, then I'd open the window.

...

That list spilled over and over and over, until I thought I might drown.

So, I opened the window for air.

...

I spent the next few years writing sad poetry, and speaking to adults about my feelings.

I was... so sad... and so lonely.

So, I learnt to put on a mask. To be brave. To be happy. To never complain.

But sometimes the list comes back.

Spilling over.

...

I don't think I'm doing eight-year-old me justice.

She did all that hard work...

All that surviving.

And I'd really like to do her justice.

Because I can't bear the thought of it all not being worth it.

...

You know, people have been trying to make adjustments to my body – to me – all my life.

And I just need someone to call time and be like "nah she's good."

And I know that person should be me.

I just cannot find the words...

And if I prayed... or wished...

I wouldn't pray to be able to walk.

Because I know that's not happening

I'd pray to be able to find those words that I cannot find.

Because that, however impossible it feels today... must be manageable. Surely?

It has to be manageable.

...

In my parents' living room there is a cabinet full of treasures.

In the middle of all these holiday souvenirs and family heirlooms, is a girl made out of clay.

It's a truly terrible piece of art.

It looks like it's corroded, but that's how she was when she was new.

I made her when I was eight

With counsellor number one.

...

I look at her.

And it's like looking in the mirror.

Like eight-year-old me has time travelled to my present and given me a message.

It's time.

I thought going back into therapy would feel like a step backwards.

But that's not true.

I'm asked to write a list of things I loved about eight-year-old me.

All the things I couldn't see at the time.

All the reasons I should have loved her more than I did.

And then I'm told to write out a list for twenty-eight year-old me.

I stress call Simon and tell him that I don't know what to write.

He offers to write a list of all the things he loves about me, if I do the same for him.

It doesn't take long for me to write...

Fun, caring, weird, spontaneous, dependable... the list goes on.

I send Simon his list, and he sends me mine.

And they are... identical.

Therapy continues and I start to cry more.

Which makes me think that she might be a terrible therapist.

But then I start to cry less.

And I figure she's a professional, she knows what she's doing.

...

Time starts to go by quicker.

I keep busy.

I bump into Justin Rogers, who tells me that he always fancied me.

Even after I pissed on him and threw up on his shoes.

Stick that on the good list.

He's married now.

...

I visit Toronto and realise why Simon moved across the ocean to be with Sophie.

Her alarm clock is the *Hello Dolly* soundtrack, and she once ran a marathon dressed up as Yoda.

One day in our car wash, I talk to Mel and let the mask fall.

We both sit there, maskless... not really knowing what to do.

It's like meeting each other for the first time.

...

Kev watches Military Wives and decides that we should all join a choir.

I can't sing for shit, but we go to the pub afterwards and it's quite fun.

Mel and I start meditating.

Mel and I stop meditating.

Mel suggests a gong bath

I suggest she goes alone.

...

I have my first one-night stand with Eric.

And it's actually alright.

I warn him about my scars, and he asks me if I have a favourite.

His top pick is the zig-zag on the back of my knee.

The division symbols on the front of my knee are mine.

So, basically my knees are banging.

And I should stop warning people about my scars.

...

I go to the annual spina bifida day clinic.

Mr Collins calls me into the consultants office, and introduces me to the medical student who'll be sitting in on my appointment.

His name's Eric and twelve hours earlier I saw his penis.

So, that's inappropriate.

Our first proper date is a silent disco.

We dance so much that Eric has to borrow an asthma pump and I spend the next few days on painkillers.

I take him to Mel's birthday BBQ.

By midnight, everyone else has headed back inside.

But Eric and I lay under our blanket, looking up at the stars.

Or rather... clouds.

But I figure that when I retell this story, there'll be stars.

He tells me about how his dad left when he was four, and that he used to practise kissing on magnums.

I tell him about my fear of rice pudding and love of silent film.

...

I take his hand.

And there is silence.

...

...

Overall, I feel like holding hands is a bit overrated.

But it's also quite nice.

...

And I know what you're thinking...

Why did you introduce the main love interest two minutes before the end of the story?

Well, this is a love story.

But it's not mine and Eric's.

Our story might be the sequel.

But let's be realistic: it could all go wrong.

Which will be crushing, but at least I could write an album of heart-rending ballads about it.

Maybe the sequel will be a musical!

But I've got to think about the budget.

...

Eric falls asleep and his hand begins to get sweaty.

...

My leg goes into spasm.

It keeps doing this recently.

I'm told it might be due to dehydration, but it could be nerve related.

I hold Eric's lovely sweaty hand and I hear Mel laughing and Kev washing up and I think about Simon and Sophie and the girl made of clay and the list and the stars...

Popular culture makes you believe that happiness is a switch.

Something happens, and that switch is triggered.

You get a promotion at work, you find God, you find your life partner, you start therapy. And that's you sorted.

And I'd like to call it bullshit.

Because it is not a switch that you suddenly find one day.

And if it is a switch, then it's temperamental and unreliable and the electrician probably needs firing.

…

I've come to realise that life can be shit and wonderful all at the same time.

It's a shit and wonderful life.

…

I'm going to end with a poem because that seems suitably wanky.

It's a short one, so please manage your expectations.

Like, literally, it's fifteen words so don't get comfortable.

Okay.

"I am happy,

I am sad,

But look to the sky, it's not so bad"

By Juno, aged eight.

   (Blackout.)

ABOUT THE AUTHOR

Amy Trigg trained at Mountview Academy of Theatre Arts. *Reasons You Should(n't) Love Me* (joint winner of the inaugural Women's Prize for Playwriting 2020) is Amy's first full length play. Amy's essay *An Ode to Improv (and Poehler and Fey)* features in the book *Feminist's Don't Wear Pink (and other lies)*. She won Colchester New Comedian of the Year 2016 for her one woman sketch *The Rebrand*. Amy is currently a writer for the upcoming BBC series *Ralph and Katie* (produced by ITV Studios) and is developing original projects for stage and screen. She has been part of the Royal Court Introduction to Playwriting Group 2020/21, BBC Drama Room 2020/21, BBC Writers Access Group 2020/21 and 4Screenwriting 2021.